I0093124

Lessons *from* LONZO

*Peace
Practices
Inspired by a
Four-Legged
Friend*

Sherry Ann Bruckner

Copyright © 2024 Sherry Ann Bruckner
Minnesota, USA

All rights reserved. You may not reproduce any contents of this book for public or private use, except for brief quotations in articles or reviews or authorized educational purposes, without the written permission of the author.

ISBN: 979-8-9894792-0-7
Ebook ISBN: 979-8-9894792-1-4
Audio ISBN: 979-8-9894792-2-1
Library of Congress Control Number: 2024900930

Foreword by Michael A. Gregory
Cover and interior design by Lucy Giller
Cover Color Pencil Sketch of Lonzo by Lyn Wanek
Edited by Ken Wachsberger

You may learn more online at: www.LessonsfromLonzo.com

I lovingly dedicate this book to the memory of Lonzo,

my furry, fun-loving, four-legged friend.

Contents

BE GENTLE WITH YOU

Lesson One: Check the Dishes 11

Lesson Two: Refill Your Bowl. 13

Lesson Three: Sniff It Out 15

Lesson Four: Ignore the Barking 17

Lesson Five: Get Your Bone. 19

Lesson Six: Release the Whimper 21

Lesson Seven: Lick Your Wounds 23

Lesson Eight: Share Your Struggles. 25

Lesson Nine: Raise Your Paw 27

Lesson Ten: Let Them Lift. 29

Lesson Eleven: Permit a Pause 31

Lesson Twelve: Take a Nap 33

Lesson Thirteen: Snuggle for Warmth 35

Lesson Fourteen: Remember to Reset 37

Lesson Fifteen: Choose Your Way 39

Lesson Sixteen: Play Every Day. 41

Lesson Seventeen: Finish Your Business. 43

Lesson Eighteen: Prance Occasionally. 45

Lesson Nineteen: Be Here Now. 47

Lesson Twenty: Allow Your Authenticity 49

Lesson Twenty-One: Hide Your Panties 51

BE GENTLE WITH ALL

Lesson Twenty-Two: Welcome People Joyfully 55

Lesson Twenty-Three: Lead with Curiosity 57

Lesson Twenty-Four: Approach with Compassion 59

Lesson Twenty-Five: Show Genuine Interest 61

Lesson Twenty-Six: Perk Your Ears. 63

Lesson Twenty-Seven: Loosen Expectations 65

Lesson Twenty-Eight: Appreciate the Awesomeness 67

Lesson Twenty-Nine: Give Love Freely 69

Lesson Thirty: Communicate Your Boundaries. 71

Lesson Thirty-One: Redirect as Needed 73

Lesson Thirty-Two: Practice Patience 75

Lesson Thirty-Three: Help Your Neighbors 77

Lesson Thirty-Four: Hold Space 79

Lesson Thirty-Five: Provide Reassurance 81

Lesson Thirty-Six: Discern Your Matches 83

Lesson Thirty-Seven: Appreciate Being Together. 85

Lesson Thirty-Eight: Gently Stand Guard 87

Lesson Thirty-Nine: Chase Wisely 89

Lesson Forty: Give Extra Grace. 91

Lesson Forty-One: Let Bygones Be 93

Lesson Forty-Two: Cherish the Humans 95

BE THE PEACE

Lesson Forty-Three: Center Your Heart 99

Lesson Forty-Four: Exist with Ease 101

Lesson Forty-Five: Lovingly Attract Love 103

Lesson Forty-Six: Frolic in Freedom 105

Lesson Forty-Seven: Relish the Path 107

Lesson Forty-Eight: Observe Your Rituals. 109

Lesson Forty-Nine: Weigh the Consequences. 111

Lesson Fifty: Go Off Leash 113

Lesson Fifty-One: Roll Over Again. 115

Lesson Fifty-Two: Be Consistently You 117

Lesson Fifty-Three: Enjoy Nature. 119

Lesson Fifty-Four: Share the Sunshine. 121

Lesson Fifty-Five: Let Ducks Be 123

Lesson Fifty-Six: Nudge the Door 125

Lesson Fifty-Seven: Accept Abundant Love. 127

Lesson Fifty-Eight: Embrace the Fullness 129

Lesson Fifty-Nine: Generate Gratitude 131

Lesson Sixty: Awaken Your Light. 133

Lesson Sixty-One: Create the Wonderful 135

Lesson Sixty-Two: Show the Way. 137

Lesson Sixty-Three: Gently Let Go. 139

Living the Lessons 141

Appreciation and Acknowledgment 143

Meet Lonzo's Human and the Author 147

Foreword

BY MICHAEL A. GREGORY

Sherry Ann Bruckner's *Lessons from Lonzo* is a heartwarming and delightful journey that invites readers to explore the profound wisdom derived from the life of her beloved four-legged companion, Lonzo. Through a series of precious and cute stories featuring Lonzo, Bruckner masterfully weaves in insightful and meaningful reflections that inspire and uplift the reader.

Bruckner's gentle and warm approach resonates effortlessly, creating an emotional connection that makes you feel like you are sharing these moments with an old friend. As you immerse yourself in the narrative, you will find not only adorable anecdotes but also valuable life lessons that transcend the boundaries between human and pet. The beauty of the book lies not just in the stories, but in the profound questions Bruckner poses, prompting readers to ponder and reflect on their own lives.

The journey is not just about Lonzo; it is about finding a more peaceful perspective through the lens of unconditional love and companionship. By the end, you will undoubtedly emerge as a better person, carrying a renewed sense of gratitude and a deeper understanding of the meaningful connections that shape our lives.

So, dive into this charming read, and let Lonzo's lessons leave an indelible mark on your heart, sparking newfound joy and contemplation.

Michael A. Gregory, a mediation and negotiation conflict resolution specialist and a professional speaker, authored 12 books including *Peaceful Resolutions, The Collaboration Effect*, and *The Servant Manager*.

Preface

As Mom and I sit at lunch, I toss out possible names for the furry four-legged critter awaiting adoption from the Lakes Area Humane Society (LAHS). Mom mentions Dad's middle name, Alonzo, and I exclaim another version: Lonzo... that is it!

Let us back up a few days though.

On April 1, 2010, I first visit LAHS. Their tag calls him Elroy. As much as I love the old TV show, *The Jetsons*, the name does not seem to fit this furry guy. The quietest among the group and full of mangled hair, this four-legged five-year old confidently crawls into my lap. We seem to simultaneously declare: We are a match. (If only my human matching could prove so simple.)

It remains no coincidence we meet during a season that marks the power of love and transformation. Lonzo's peaceful presence opens space for tremendous love and plays a significant role in my own transformation.

Prior to his passing on June 15, 2021, I begin writing the ways Lonzo inspires me to be gentler with myself, gentler with the people around me, and, overall, more at peace and peaceful. His teachings slowly evolve into this book, *Lessons from Lonzo*. I am now ready to share his spirit in hopes it brings similar healing to your heart, smiles to your soul, and the comfort of personal peace.

Introduction

Whether you share your home with a four-legged friend or prefer to spend your time with less furry critters, *Lessons from Lonzo* invites you to consider your own peace.

Peace is not a one-and-done activity. Practicing peace takes practice.

These practices inspired by Lonzo allow you to consider yourself, your relationship with those around you, and who you choose to be. They fall under three core premises.

BE GENTLE WITH YOU

As Lonzo is gentle with himself, may you also be gentle with you.

Being gentle with you involves both laughter (Hide Your Panties) and love (Lick Your Wounds). You begin by noticing when one of your cups in life might call for a refill. By acknowledging your own basic needs and wishes, you may frame a plan to take care of yourself. This care from being gentle provides a sense of inner peace. Inner peace creates the foundation for outer peace.

May you be gentle with you.

BE GENTLE WITH ALL

Lonzo enters my life with history, which remains his own story. It proves easy to be gentle with him because he maintains a gentle disposition. Being gentle with a cute, sweet, furry four-legged friend serves as a reminder that I am able to be gentle. It is a choice in every moment.

Each human you encounter brings their own history as well. Their story, her story, and his story may have similarities and differences which shape who they are and how they show up. The same gentleness Lonzo offers to humans, and I offer to him, may be given to any human at any time and in any place.

Being gentle remains a choice.

May you be gentle with all.

BE THE PEACE

Lonzo glides gracefully through his days. This does not mean he does not protect himself or his space. He does so, however, in a way that he does not become the aggressor. Regardless of any challenging circumstances in a particular moment, Lonzo seems to know exactly who he is and how he will show up in the world.

You choose the energy you bring to each moment. You may demonstrate self-respect and hold firm to your values while showing up as a person who reflects value for all humanity in your very being.

You may be whoever and however you wish to be.

May you be the peace.

I invite you to keep this book nearby and refer to it time and again. May you uncover your own sense of inner peace along the way and begin to live from these core messages.

Be gentle with you. Be gentle with all. Be the peace.

Be Gentle *with* You

Check the Dishes

Lonzo's two dog dishes receive multiple visits from him throughout the day. I also give them a glance multiple times to check on what he may need. If he notices their emptiness before I do, he simply lies in front of the dish. Of course, the dishes only signal his sustenance needs. He makes known his wishes to go outside, receive snuggle time, and play after we both check the dishes.

You may be the only one checking your own dishes. If you are like many adults, you maintain primary responsibility for monitoring your own well-being. This extends beyond food and water to rest, laughter and play, love, support, and connection. When your basic needs go unmet, it impacts your level of inner peace. Remember to check your own dishes.

What happens when your needs go unnoticed?

What happens when you pay attention to you?

What are your plans to check your own dishes?

Refill Your Bowl

Lonzo's bowls rarely sit empty. As he nibbles on his food throughout the day and clenches his thirst at his leisure, he enjoys a healthy abundance. His bowls receive a refill of water or food at least twice each day. He receives consistent amounts to maintain his own health.

Knowing your level of fullness and doing something about it require two different skills—awareness and action. It is up to you to take the time to refill. When you plan ways to do so daily or weekly, it proves easier to replenish. While it might seem manageable to run on low or empty for a while, it eventually takes a toll. Remember to refill your bowl regularly.

🐾   *What happens when you do not refill your bowls?*

🐾   *What are your plans to replenish and refill regularly?*

🐾   *What time are you setting aside for you?*

Sniff It Out

Lonzo gets his nose into so much...shoes, purses, coats, random objects in the grass. He gives it all his gentle sniff test. His curiosity keeps him sniffing until he has enough information. This allows him to decide what receives his further time, energy, and attention. He takes care of himself when he sniffs it out.

As you get curious about what you observe, you may use your own set of sniff tests to help you gain more information. A deeper understanding allows you to decide whether to invest further time, energy, and attention here. It may or may not be a fit for you at this moment or in this space. You do not know until you sniff it out.

🐾 *What is your sniff test?*

🐾 *What happens when you do not use it?*

🐾 *What happens when you take time to sniff it out?*

Ignore the Barking

Some dogs bark as soon as they see a person or critter, or for reasons unknown. Upon hearing another bark, Lonzo typically keeps going at the same pace in the same direction with little or no interest in the barker. He does not allow a little outside noise to interrupt him or change his path.

Hearing people's comments and thoughts may lead you to question your path. You may begin to think you must change who you are or what you do. Of course, you may wish to remain aware of signs, warnings, or suggestions for ways of living that better serve you. You need not, however, pay attention to outside noise from all sources all the time. You may choose when to listen or simply ignore the barking.

🐾 *What power do you give away?*

🐾 *Under what circumstances will you listen to outside thoughts and opinions?*

🐾 *What happens when you ignore the barking?*

Get Your Bone

The scent of the beef bone under the neighbors' deck fills the air. Lonzo hunkers in as close as he can, yet it eludes him as he rests inside for the night allured by smells through an open window.

With a new day upon him, Lonzo steps out the back door. He bolts across the yard, scurries below their deck, and claims his prize. He remembers exactly what he wants and goes for it with greater focus. Just because he could not have his bone yesterday does not prevent him from getting it today.

When you do not get what you want, you may start to believe it is not for you. It may not be. Whether your dream comes true does not depend upon one denial, rejection, or setback. Yesterday's result becomes today's starting point, and you begin it with the knowledge, experience, and wisdom from yesterday. Keep taking steps toward your vision if you really wish to get your bone.

🐾 *What prize bone do you envision?*

🐾 *What is your level of desire to attain it?*

🐾 *What time and energy will you put into it?*

Release the Whimper

On the rare occasion when Lonzo experiences pain, he lets out a whimper. He allows himself to express his feelings of hurt. He releases his sadness and pain in the moment. He does not let the pain build before releasing it and then act as the aggressor, spreading his discontent onto anyone else. He honors his own feelings and chooses to release the whimper.

When you do not let yourself feel, your feelings may end up taking control of you and then come out in ways that further harm you, your relationships, or both. Avoiding or stuffing feelings with food, alcohol, busyness, or some other escape only serves to delay.

You get to feel what you feel. Letting yourself feel allows you to reclaim your personal power. You honor your own humanity when you release the whimper.

What grace do you allow yourself to feel?

What practices help you face your feelings?

What happens when you release the whimper?

Lick Your Wounds

When Lonzo hurts his paw, he licks it. He takes time to nurture and care for himself. He is not too busy or caught up in what someone else might think to lick his paw. His own well-being matters. He takes the time to lick his wounds and care for himself.

When you hurt, you, too, may pause and care for yourself. Whether the wound be physical, emotional, or spiritual, it calls for your attention. Believing something or someone else holds more importance and neglecting yourself creates consequences.

When you care for yourself, you show that your health and well-being matter. Remember to take time for self-care and lick your wounds as needed.

What does licking your wounds mean to you?

What happens when you do not prioritize your own wounds?

What steps will you take to prioritize your own health and well-being?

Share Your Struggles

Unaware of Lonzo's whereabouts, a sharp whine floating down the hall from the spare bedroom quickly informs me. While in there a few moments earlier, Lonzo enters without my noticing.

As I check on him and open the door, my four-legged friend rushes past me and down the hall. He does not like this confinement and his voice tells me so. If he does not express himself, I do not know that he struggles for help.

In any relationship, you may experience hurt or disappointment. Your people may not know you are hurting unless you tell them.

Notifying folks of your needs lightens your emotional burden. When you keep your whines or wishes to yourself, you find frustration and disappointment. You create deeper connections when you share your struggles.

🐾 *What happens when you feel hurt or shut out?*

🐾 *What steps might you take to create more connections?*

🐾 *What happens when you share your struggles?*

Raise Your Paw

As the snowbanks line the yards and ice covers the streets, Lonzo's desire for the normal neighborhood stroll becomes a bit less pleasant for him. As we loop back toward home, he simply stops and lifts his front paw. His paw lift serves as my invitation to lift and carry him.

Eventually, he wiggles enough to let me know he may now walk on his own. He asks for help when he wants it. His winter walks grow more comfortable when he raises his paw.

Perhaps, you do not like asking for help. You may hold certain beliefs about vulnerability and independence. You may believe you are capable of taking on tasks by yourself. You might believe you must always carry yourself. It is okay to raise your paw and ask for help.

🐾 *What is your level of comfort in asking for help?*

🐾 *What prevents you from asking?*

🐾 *What happens when you ask for help?*

Let Them Lift

On icy Minnesota days, Lonzo allows me to carry him down the slippery frozen street. When the spring thaw arrives and his underbelly becomes a mud vacuum, he also gets an escort through the house straight into the bathtub. It makes the experience easier and more enjoyable for both of us when he lets me lift him.

Asking for help and then accepting it may prove different undertakings. You may unconsciously resist offers of assistance even as you seek assistance.

Letting people help you not only helps you. It also allows someone else to experience the joy and satisfaction that comes with being the helper. It benefits everyone involved when you sometimes let them lift.

What does it mean to let them lift?

Who benefits when you accept help?

To what extent are you open to accepting?

Permit a Pause

As he nears the end of his life, Lonzo simply stops in the middle of the street or driveway. It is as if to say, "This is as far as I am able to go." Somedays, I wait. When he is ready, he starts moving again. Other days, I carry him the rest of the way. When he reaches his own limits, Lonzo permits a pause.

You may have times when you wish to keep going. Having more to do or take care of may seem the permanent reality. Tasks could fill life 24/7.

After a certain amount of time, the law of diminishing returns comes into play. The human body, mind, and spirit cannot keep going and doing without a proper break. Give yourself some time and permit a pause.

🐾 *What happens when you push yourself to keep going?*

🐾 *What would it mean to take a break?*

🐾 *What happens when you permit a pause?*

Take a Nap

While Lonzo enjoys his walks, he also loves his naps. He naps increasingly more as he ages. He just as easily snuggles on the couch, in his bed, or on a random person's coat.

Most soft items on the floor equal a bed in Lonzo's world. If it is fluffy and free, he claims it as a resting place. He honors his body and takes a nap, whenever and wherever.

Your body may call out to you for rest. The call may start as a small whisper or a gentle nudge. When you do not honor your body's wishes, they grow louder and louder.

Whether lying ten minutes on the couch, catching a full-on bed sleep, or softening your gaze while sitting upright in a chair, rest restores the body and the mind. Everything else may wait, will wait, simply does not have to be done now, or perhaps at all. When the body calls for rest, take a nap.

What happens when your body calls for rest?

How much rest time do you allow yourself?

What happens when you honor your body by taking a nap?

Snuggle for Warmth

Lonzo nestles near my feet as I stretch out on the couch. His weight secures the blanket to my feet. He stretches his body in such a way that my lower legs feel warmth. Sometimes, he looks so comfortable I do not wish to move. While he snuggles for warmth, I am also comfortable and cozy.

You may have a person, critter, or blanket that brings you cuddling comfort. It may warm your body, comfort your mind, or soothe your soul. Nuzzling up may slow your heartbeat, allowing your whole body to relax. You may wish to snuggle for warmth of your body, heart, or both.

🐾 *Where do you like to snuggle?*

🐾 *What happens when you nestle somewhere?*

🐾 *What feelings occur when you snuggle?*

Remember to Reset

When Lonzo takes a nap or pauses, he lets go of his tired, worn-out energy. Naps and pauses serve the purpose of breaking up the current energy. They offer him an opportunity to recharge. He leaves his tiredness and worn-out energy where he pauses and brings fresh energy into the new moment. He remembers to reset.

How you spend your time when you take a pause matters. You may sometimes give yourself *breaks* that do not serve to rejuvenate or refresh you. You may choose activities that further drain you physically or emotionally, or you may choose activities that help you reset. If you take the time for a break, pay attention to whether it restores your energy. Remember to reset.

What does remember to reset mean to you?

What allows you to best rejuvenate and refresh?

What happens when you remember to reset?

Choose Your Way

Lonzo might fetch two or three times, and then show no further interest. I do not force him to fetch, nor could I. Lonzo may choose a certain toy one day and another toy a different day. Some days he wants to be alone on his bed; other days he interacts with all the humans. He chooses his way.

Your ideas about connection, joy, and meaning may not be the same as those around you. You may decide what this looks like to you. You get to live your life as you wish. You may choose when, where, and whether you engage in any activity.

Your choices may determine who is willing to be with you, and that is okay. You may change your mind sometimes, too, which is acceptable. You may choose your way.

What does it mean to choose your way?

Which of your ways works best for you?

What happens when you choose your way?

Play Every Day

Lonzo's toys begin the morning in a basket. Later, a few may show up by the front door, another on the rug, and a couple by his bed. He leaves regular evidence that he plays with (or at least moves) his toys. He does so without reminders or prompting. He naturally chooses to play every day.

Your calendar may allow time for activities or hobbies that spark joy. You may fill your moments with experiences that do not bring pure joy (scrolling through social media, contemplating calories). You may mindlessly neglect opportunities that fully light you up. Your heart sings with a sense of joy when you remember to play every day.

What feels like playing to you?

What time do you allow yourself to play?

What happens in you when you remember to play every day?

Finish Your Business

When the temperature hits minus forty in Minnesota, Lonzo's desire to go outside hits zero. Whether out of respect for himself or me, he confronts the freezing air, takes only a few steps, and quickly cares for his personal business. Delaying would only create more discomfort. Lonzo quickly re-enters the house and goes about his day. He knows what must be done and finishes his business.

Sometimes, you may avoid or delay working on a certain project. Yet, you still give time and energy to thinking about it. Thinking certainly plays a key role in planning a project, yet you must also act.

Procrastination prevents progress. In the time it takes you to delay, you might simply complete the task and relieve the discomfort. You may move onto another project you love even more when you finish your business.

🐾   *What are you delaying?*

🐾   *What are the costs of not finishing?*

🐾   *What happens when you finish your business?*

Prance Occasionally

Lonzo prances down the street with his chin up. He holds himself in dignity and grace of one the biggest dogs in the neighborhood even though he is one of the smallest. He behaves obliviously to his own size and stature relative to the creatures around him. He does not act better than any dog; he does act as though no dog is better than him. He struts his stuff and prances occasionally.

Notice your breath and feel your heartbeat. You are a human being with the same level of intrinsic value as any other human being. Whether anyone else recognizes your worth does not change your value. You choose whether you honor your own dignity and grace at any time in any place. Go ahead and prance occasionally.

What do you believe about you?

What situations cause you to believe this?

What happens when you allow yourself to prance occasionally?

Be Here Now

Lonzo appears to be fully present wherever he is in the moment. When he tugs at a toy, it is as though that toy represents the only thing in the world. When lying in the backyard, he may be fully captivated by a bird or another critter. Lonzo appears fully present in each moment. He tends to be wherever he is.

So many distractions may remove you from the present moment. A sound, a sight, or a memory may take you from where you are right now to some other place or time. Thoughts may carry you between the past or future with occasional stops in the present.

When you notice your breath enter and exit your body, you return to the present moment. You may stay right here right now. You only have one chance to be fully present in this present moment. Be here now.

What keeps you from being fully where you are?

What helps you stay in the present moment?

What happens when you choose to be right here right now?

Allow Your Authenticity

Most people who meet Lonzo instantaneously love him. He just is who he is. He maintains his own spirit. He does not change himself to appease. It would be unfortunate for him to be anything or anyone other than this beautiful spirit in this fury four-legged form. He allows his own authenticity.

You may think you must behave in a certain way to fit in. You get to be the fullest, truest version of you that aligns with your own inner light. You belong in this world at this exact time exactly as you are. Your people will be drawn to you. They may be waiting for you to show up as you. Allow your authenticity.

What does it mean to allow your authenticity?

Where do you feel most free to be you?

What happens when you allow you to be you?

Hide Your Panties

Overnight guests hear, "Hide your panties." Lonzo's proclivity and strong urge to find the sacred clothing do not discriminate. If he senses them within sniff shot, he does not care what style or type they are. He finds a way to chew on panties, boxers, or briefs.

His Uncle People give him a dog tag for Christmas that appropriately reads "Panty Bandit." Thankfully, we find humor, as Lonzo offers another reminder to hide the panties.

No matter how many warning flags or reminders you receive, you may occasionally overlook something important to you. No matter how careful you are, events just happen beyond your control. While it may seem serious, you may look for the hidden humor. You may choose to laugh off life's mishaps and remember to hide your panties better next time.

What level of seriousness do you bring to the world?

Where do you find humor in life?

What happens when you laugh off life's mishaps?

Be Gentle
with All

Welcome People Joyfully

Lonzo genuinely enjoys seeing people and critters. He offers a joyful welcome to most everyone he encounters. His tail wags excitedly as he awaits their approach. When they come near, he takes the first step and sniffs around their ankles, or he jumps with glee. He warms many hearts with his joyful welcome.

Furry four-leggeds often seem excited to see other four-leggeds. Humans tend to show less excitement when encountering fellow humans. If you see or hear a human "Wow," you get to experience a moment with this human. You may know nothing about their day or their life experiences.

If you hold enough joy, you may spread it through a smile, "hello," or hug. Welcoming people joyfully brings joy.

What does welcoming joyfully look like to you?

What does it feel like when someone welcomes you joyfully?

What happens when you joyfully welcome one person?

Lead with Curiosity

Lonzo sniffs the same mailbox pole and trees thousands of times. He does not presume they remain exactly as they were even earlier in the day. No matter how often something gets his sniff test, he still sniffs it the next time he encounters it. He opens his mind to the possibility that it might be different. It may or may not be the same as last time. He leads with curiosity.

You may form opinions or ideas about people and think you know everything there is to know about them. Yet, humans experience different encounters and situations every day that may impact who they are or how they perceive and interact.

This means the person may or may not think, speak, or act the same as yesterday or last year. When you look a little closer or question deeper, you learn more. You expand your mind when you lead with curiosity.

What does it mean to lead with curiosity?

What happens when you let go of assumptions?

Where could you practice more curiosity?

Approach with Compassion

When Lonzo gets to a door and it remains only slightly open, he pauses. He also seems hesitant around screen doors. Although his body could fit through the opening in the outside doorway, he hesitates until it is fully open.

While this behavior may not make sense, it prompts me to wonder what causes his hesitancy. His hesitancy leads me to approach him with compassion.

You might notice folks do or say things that you do not understand. Even when you know someone well, you do not know all their stories and experiences. So many experiences shape who you are, and what you think, say, and do. The same holds true for your fellow humans. When you approach with compassion, you open space for understanding.

What leads you to think, say, and do as you think, say, and do?

What might be behind the behavior of the people around you?

What happens when you approach with compassion?

Show Genuine Interest

Lonzo shows interest in and receives attention from many people, and a few critters along his journey. People often ask about his well-being. His interest in who and what is around him demonstrates a level of care. People resonate with Lonzo's nature because he shows genuine interest.

When you show interest in who or what matters to the people in your life, you express a level of care and concern. You do this by, for instance, asking about someone's life experience with attentiveness. You go deeper than asking the offhand-ed, often rhetorical "How are you?" You ask questions that demonstrate a willingness to learn. You show genuine caring about another's well-being, and interest in their personhood.

🐾 *What questions reflect genuine care to you?*

🐾 *What happens when someone shows interest in your life and well-being?*

🐾 *What might happen if you ask questions to understand one person better this week?*

Perk Your Ears

Lonzo's ears perk up at the sound of a loved one's vehicle, or the voice on the other end of the phone. He senses changes in my tone of voice too. Lonzo understands the playfulness, seriousness, or somberness of a moment. He gains so much information and prepares for interactions when he perks his ears.

While words offer information, volume, speed, and inflection also offer valuable insight. When you listen closely, you sense what someone might be feeling.

Feelings signal whether someone believes their needs are met. Joy and contentment suggest needs are met. Anger or sadness send the message of unmet needs.

Understanding the connection between feelings and needs, you may listen closely for cues. To better prepare for conversations, perk your ears.

What does it mean to listen for feelings?

How often do you listen for the underlying message?

What happens when you perk your ears?

Loosen Expectations

When Lonzo hears a loved one's vehicle or voice, he looks for them and expects them to enter a certain door. He may find the person standing outside, entering another door, or not even near the house. As their voice travels over the airways through the phone and he discovers they are not there, Lonzo bounces back to his peaceful self as he loosens his expectations.

A part of you may feel disappointment when circumstances do not turn out as expected. As you loosen your grip on how things "should be," you may certainly experience frustration or even sadness.

Human experience sometimes involves change or the unexpected. You may choose to hold onto expectations or lean into the reality of what exists. You realize the temporariness of the current situation as you loosen expectations.

What happens when you hold fast to expectations?

What happens when you loosen expectations?

What expectations might you loosen?

Appreciate the Awesomeness

Lonzo shares character traits with some dogs yet remains quite different from others. His coloring, size, and actions may be alike or unique. The neighborhood feels richer and more beautiful with dogs of diverse sizes, shapes, colors, and demeanors. The fact that all these four-legged friends exist is marvelous. While recognizing their commonality, I marvel at the unique awesomeness of each critter.

No other human on earth is exactly like you. You are a unique, one-of-a-kind being. As you learn differing ideas, beliefs, and behaviors, you allow expansion. Various body types, skin tones, cultures, and religions increase the richness and fullness of the human experience. You may embrace both the common humanity, and the unique differences in this human experience. You may choose to appreciate the awesomeness.

🐾 *What do you notice as the benefits of people being different from each other?*

🐾 *How do you support each human's uniqueness?*

🐾 *What happens when you appreciate the awesomeness of humanity?*

Give Love Freely

Lonzo does not have to do anything for me to love him. Simply being Lonzo proves more than enough. Lonzo loves people. The people do not have to do anything to earn Lonzo's love. He often knows nothing about them. He senses their essence, an inherent worthiness of love, and chooses to give love freely.

You cannot and do not earn love. Folks around you may choose whether to love. Their willingness to love you as you wish to be loved holds no reflection on you or your lovability.

You may always choose love. You may distinguish loving from giving time and energy. Loving may involve sending loving energy from a distance. You may always give love freely.

🐾 *Who or what receives your time and energy?*

🐾 *What level of love do you share?*

🐾 *What happens when you give love freely?*

Communicate Your Boundaries

Most everyone describes Lonzo as the sweetest dog. He is. As you read, you may realize he loves people, friends, families, and strangers alike. When one person visits, however, Lonzo barks and barks. Lonzo's tone does not seem angry. It does, however, send a clear message as he stands his ground and communicates his boundaries.

Healthy boundaries flow from a place of values, including valuing yourself and your fellow humans. When you draw lines, you do not demand specific behavior. The lines inform folks how you will respond to certain behavior.

You show respect when you let someone know with calm confidence what behaviors you find acceptable and will allow in advance, rather than creating rules and penalties that may not fit the violation after the fact. You may clearly and compassionately communicate your boundaries.

What values determine your boundaries?

How do you communicate your boundaries?

What respect do you show for the boundaries of people around you?

Redirect as Needed

As Lonzo starts to dig through the trash bag, I simply remove it from his reach. Sometimes his paws turn toward items that may not be easily moved. In those moments, I must redirect his attention. Calling his name or enticing him with a squeaky toy takes his focus off the litter that does not serve him.

When your thoughts turn to past hurts, you may allow yourself moments to grieve. Thoughts may return to places of pain, or ideas that do not serve who you wish to be, or where you wish to go. It is neither right nor wrong to think these thoughts. Notice if your thoughts serve who you are and who you wish to be. You may redirect your thoughts as needed.

What thoughts do you notice?

What thoughts align with who you wish to be?

What thoughts would it be helpful to redirect?

Practice Patience

Lonzo takes his time taking care of his business. Days when I seem preoccupied with a "to-do" list, he chooses to take a little longer, as if to say, "Patience, why the hurry?" When I adopt the attitude that this time is his time and it will take how long it takes, he seems more at ease and takes less time to take care of his business. Lonzo reminds me to practice patience.

You may find yourself hurrying through life with a lengthening to-do list. The term "human being" reminds you to "be." You do not have to rush, rush, rush, or do, do, do. You may simply be. By releasing the doing and opening space for being, you practice patience.

What does patience look like to you?

What happens when you practice patience?

What happens when you focus on "being" rather than "doing?"

Help Your Neighbors

Lonzo's custom of going outside at least every morning, noon, afternoon, and evening occurs even without my presence. While most times I plan my away times in advance to coordinate his care, gracious neighbors come to the rescue with my last-minute calls for help. The kindness of neighbors time and again offers such relief and peace of mind and creates connection in the community.

Whether you help someone open a door, lift a box or refrigerator, or check on their four-legged friend, your gift of time eases the load. Your willingness to help someone for five minutes or five hours offers support and provides a sense of relief that you may not even realize. It creates a sense of connection, as you take turns helping each other out as needed. You make the community a better place when you help your neighbors.

What sense of connection do you find in helping?

What happens when folks help you?

How might you help your neighbors?

Hold Space

Lonzo sees me through many seasons of life...from meal prep, joyful laughter, singing, and playing; to days of full-on grief and blotchy-face sobbing; and everything in between. He appears comfortable sitting near me in any experience. He does not need to fix it. Just being there makes a difference. He holds space for me to be me.

When you hold space for someone, you allow them to be who they are and feel what they feel. You do not have to fix it or say anything. You may allow a grieving friend to cry while you are on the other end of the telephone line, or sit in comfortable supportive silence as a loved one processes a situation. You may honor someone's truth as you hold space.

What does holding space mean to you?

What happens when you hold space for someone?

What do you feel when someone holds space for you?

Provide Reassurance

Occasionally, Lonzo barks and barks as soon as I leave his visibility. He simply needs reassurance, because when I say, "I'm over here, buddy," he seems okay. Other times, I physically go to him to let him know I am there. He shows relief when I provide reassurance.

Some days you may need reassurance. While a part of you sends the message of "Give me space," another part of you may still wish to know that someone cares.

The folks around you may be experiencing similar emotions. You may offer a comforting word or a hug. Acknowledging people with simple gestures of kindness tells them they are not alone. You provide reassurance.

What does reassurance look like to you?

What happens when you offer reassurance?

What happens when you receive reassurance?

Discern Your Matches

Lonzo rarely meets a tree he does not check out before taking care of personal business. It must be just the right match. It strikes me that he still checks out his "regular" trees as though deciding whether each one remains a good fit. Whether or not he chooses a particular tree does not make the tree good or bad; he simply discerns his match.

Certain places, spaces, or people may not be a match for you. It does not make anyone "right" or "wrong" or "good" or "bad." It just may not be a match right now, today, or ever. People, jobs, and homes have different matches. You will not be a fit for everyone and everything, nor will everyone or everything be a fit for you. You may discern your matches.

🐾 *What helps you discern your matches?*

🐾 *What do you do when something or someone no longer matches?*

🐾 *What happens when you discern without judgment or labels?*

Appreciate Being Together

Lonzo taps his neck on the top of my left arm as his way of requesting that I lower it. It must be in a certain position for his neck to rest perfectly in the crook of my elbow. He tends to find the bends in my knee and ankle for his resting spots as well. Seeing him so comfortable brings a smile to my face. We both appreciate being together.

You may experience millions of moments in a lifetime. You may sense that you must go or do or give for human relationships to be special. At the core, humans are relational beings with basic needs for love and support. Comfort comes from the connection of sharing this human experience. As you take this journey through life with your fellow humans, you may simply appreciate being together.

What do you appreciate about your relationships?

What does appreciate being together mean to you?

In what ways will you show people you appreciate being together?

LESSON THIRTY-EIGHT

Gently Stand Guard

Lonzo stays on the main floor of our rambler home. He never ever ventures to the lower level until this one time. As I lead a furnace repair person downstairs, I find Lonzo trotting down the stairs with us. He keeps a close eye on this stranger. Lonzo does not do anything. His presence, while surprising, shows his willingness to guard me.

You may have myriad thoughts about what it means to protect people. It may be about keeping folks physically safe with secure housing and clean drinking water. You may focus on uplifting their level of joy and well-being. You might understand the importance of paying attention to emotions. You may stand up for people in a way that says, "I care. I am here for you." Gently stand guard for people.

What helps you feel safe and protected?

In what ways do you protect people?

What does it mean to gently stand guard?

Chase Wisely

Even as a young pup, Lonzo shares little interest in chasing other critters. He might let out a bark at the occasional rabbit (for which I am grateful because I do not want rabbits munching on the veggies). He may chase through the yard to get a bone. Lonzo remains selective about what receives his time and energy. He chases wisely.

You may give a great deal of time, energy, and attention to a relationship or activity. You may receive a connection, joy, meaning, or purpose from doing so. The level at which you give and receive may ebb and flow. You hold authority over your life. You may choose when, where, or how to invest your time, energy, and attention. When you know what you really wish to go after, you chase wisely.

What do you find yourself chasing?

What happens when you stop chasing?

What does chasing wisely mean to you?

Give Extra Grace

Lonzo stands in front of the door. He does not bark or whine. His tail wags in anticipation. It is clearly time. He sees me pulling on my boots and snow pants. Going for morning walks in the winter takes a little more preparation time on my part. I am not ready as quickly as he is. Lonzo gives extra grace.

Throughout life you encounter people with various levels of skill or preparedness in a situation. You, too, bring different skillsets and understandings to various moments. Humans grasp concepts and ideas at differing paces. You, too, learn at a different pace. Someone offers you grace as you learn to speak, walk, read, write, and attempt various life skills. Give extra grace to everyone.

What does giving extra grace mean to you?

What happens when you receive grace?

What happens when you give extra grace?

Let Bygones Be

In Lonzo's world, what happens in the past stays in the past. (Unless, of course, bone under the neighbors' deck beckons). While he may sometimes express discontent in not getting a treat when he wants it or in being left home alone, he does not hold a grudge. He engages me with the same exuberance regardless of the last encounter.

You may carry many memories of times you wish to repeat and others you may prefer not. Reflecting on the past may give you valuable information to move forward in your chosen direction. You may choose to bring forward the lessons and let the rest go. You may find purpose without carrying the pain. You may choose what, if any, power you give to events from years, weeks, or moments in the past. You may let bygones be.

What parts of the past do you carry forward?

What parts of your past may you let go?

What bygones could you let be?

Cherish the Humans

As I pull into the driveway, Lonzo's little face peeks through the living room window with his front legs up on the lower windowsill. As soon as he sees my car, he beelines to the garage entry. Whether I am away for three days or three minutes, each time I enter the room, Lonzo greets me with first-time enthusiasm. He similarly jumps up with excitement upon visits from his Grandma Person, Uncle People, and special friends, as if to say, "Yippee, my person is here." No matter how long between visits, Lonzo cherishes the humans.

You may be less inclined to show too much excitement in encountering another human. Perhaps, you now greet long-time friends with slight screeches of excitement, due to the distance between visits. How you express yourself in any human encounter transforms the energy in the relationship.

When opportunities arise, you may remind someone how special they are, or at least that they matter. You typically do not know this is the last interaction, until after the interaction. Remember to cherish humans.

How do you let people know they matter?

When do you feel valued in your relationships?

What happens when cherish the humans?

Be *the* Peace

Center Your Heart

Lonzo may stay close by my side or roam his space, whether in the house or outdoors. He may choose to stay close for connection or venture off to enjoy his own freedom. He knows where he feels called to be. Lonzo simply follows his heart.

Your heart may call you toward connection, creativity, or freedom. As you pay closer attention to you, you learn whether to engage immediately or wait to respond to invitations. You know what aligns with inner peace. Sense what it means to listen to your heart. When you notice your breath as it flows with your heartbeat, you center your heart.

Where does your heart lead you?

What does it mean for you to follow your heart?

What happens when you follow your heart?

Exist with Ease

In our early days together, Lonzo nudges me awake at 5 a.m. to go outside. Nearer the end of his time on earth, I wake him at 7:30 a.m. He chooses how much he sleeps. Some days, he may walk through the entire neighborhood. Other days, he leads me across the street and turns around toward home. He does not push himself. He exists with ease.

Sometimes in life, you may experience a pull to do this or that or feel you must go, do, and accomplish. Spending so much time pushing to "get things done" or "make it happen," you may miss the underlying reason for being or doing.

Attempting to force yourself to go or be a certain way rarely feels positive for anyone involved. You may simply take steps in the direction you wish to go and exist with ease.

What does exist with ease mean to you?

What level of ease do you allow in your existence?

In what ways might you create more ease?

Lovingly Attract Love

Lonzo's spirit allows for constant sweet, loving, and joyful encounters. He brings smiles to so many. Lonzo loves himself and most everyone he encounters. People love him, too. I hear the true love in the tone of their voices as folks say "Loonzo-ooooo." Lonzo's loving self attracts more love.

When you love yourself and the people you encounter, it shows. If you hold onto love and do not share it with anyone, you cut off the circulation. The more love you give, the more love you receive.

You choose who you love and how much love you share in the world. Your love may not attract a specific person you wish to have in your life. You may attract love in a different form. Your love attracts love at the level of your openness to give and receive love. Your love attracts love.

What amount of love do you share?

What level of love are you open to receiving?

What connection do you notice between the levels of love you give and receive?

Frolic in Freedom

Lonzo embraces the joy of snow more than ever when on the frozen lake. It offers him so much freedom to race without restriction. His furriness gleefully bounces through the powder on the ice-covered water. The snow flies over and around him as the air pins his ears back against his head. He fully frolics in freedom.

Times of feeling excited to move about may occur less regularly as an adult. Whether you believe yourself free to be whoever you wish remains a thought within yourself. You remain free to think as you choose. Each moment you may choose who and how to be. This time is your time. You may choose to frolic in freedom.

What does frolicking mean to you?

What does freedom feel like to you?

What happens when you frolic in freedom?

Relish the Path

Lonzo takes his sweet time on any path he finds himself. He savors deer in the distant woods, tiny caterpillars on a limb, or gum wrappers in the grass. Even when he runs, he does not seem to be in a rush. He just moves with more speed.

He does not push or force. Not beholden to anyone else's pace of life or the rush of the world around him, Lonzo embraces his own slower pace. He knows that all paths lead home. He relishes the path.

You may rush to finish a task and move on to the next. Always in a hurry to get something done, you may overlook the importance of the process. You miss the joy of the path. The end of the path arrives when it arrives. You need not be in any rush to get there. You may simply relish the path.

Where are you on your path?

What do you notice when you take your time?

What does it mean for you to relish the path?

Observe Your Rituals

Lonzo strides to his bed, paws at it three times, and walks in a small circle before lying down. He eats at certain times and tends to rest at certain other times. Observing rituals and ways of being offers a sense of comfort or security. While observing him observe his rituals, I wonder how he began to observe these rituals.

You may have certain ways of doing or being in the world that you find perfectly valid, or that you may not even notice. Someone else watching may wonder why or question whether your actions make sense.

Some practices set you up for success; others may detract from it. Of course, rituals may provide peace of mind. When you really wonder about and observe your own rituals, you may decide whether you really wish to continue observing them.

What rituals do you observe?

What does it mean for a ritual to be life-giving, uplifting, and affirming of who you wish to be?

Which rituals call for adjustment or replacement?

Weigh the Consequences

Lonzo gobbles up a cheese platter left unattended. He enjoys the short-term benefit of seizing the opportunity. He lacks the ability to know or understand the resulting sickness and bodily discomfort. Recognizing both short-term and long-term impact matters. It proves important to weigh the consequences.

You, too, may not always consider the long-term consequences of your actions. While the earlier version of you may think something sounds lovely, the five-minute-, five-week-, or five-year-later version of you disagrees.

When you consider whether actions align with who you wish to be and where you wish to go, potential outcomes help you weigh the choice. Considering short-term and long-term consequences matters. Weighing consequences increases inner peace and reduces outer conflict.

- *What are the immediate and lasting effects of your decisions?*

- *What appeals to you in the short-term, and less so in the long-term?*

- *What happens when you weigh the consequences?*

Go Off Leash

A leash usually keeps Lonzo within a certain distance when outside. This rule protects both four-legged fury friends and the two-leggeds who typically accompany them. With the lake frozen over, or when he bolts out the door before me, he gets to go off leash. At least for a bit, rule breaking occurs, and Lonzo delights in this rarity. It causes no harm to anyone, and no foreseeable risk of harm. On occasion, it is okay to go off leash.

You may view rules as hard, fast, and always to be followed. You might see them as recommendations, guidelines, or suggestions. You perhaps find it acceptable to break rules and resent it when others do so, or vice versa. Understanding the reason behind the rule, you may discern when and under what circumstances you might bend or break it. If you are not causing harm to yourself or anyone else, you may go off leash occasionally.

What does following the rules mean to you?

Under what circumstances do you find it acceptable to break them?

What happens if you go off leash occasionally?

Roll Over Again

Lonzo shares his home with me for months before he reveals his knowledge and ability to roll over. Gathered for a game night, a friend's son signals Lonzo to roll over. Lonzo rolls over. I did not know he could do this and never thought to use the signal or ask him.

Lonzo demonstrates his understanding of this skill repeatedly upon request. He seems to enjoy performing this maneuver. I signal and he rolls over again.

You may have gifts and talents that you do not share with anyone else or remain unaware they exist. You may not even know your own capabilities unless or until you attempt.

You also do not know the capacity of any human being or any other member of creation. You may decide what you believe they are capable of without full awareness of their beautiful, wonderful talents within.

What keeps you from sharing your gifts and talents?

How do you uplift others to share theirs?

What happens when you invite someone else to show their talents?

Be Consistently You

While sometimes Lonzo may act in ways a bit out of the ordinary (enter Panty Bandit), he creates consistent character traits. He tends to be gentle with himself and with the rest of creation. He tends to be a peaceful being. He maintains predictable mannerisms by being his own being while doing whatever he happens to be doing. Lonzo remains consistently Lonzo.

You may not always be able to choose what happens to you, or what life experiences come your way. You may always choose who you are. You may choose in advance what character traits you wish to exhibit.

Who you are being matters much more than what you are doing. When you act in alignment with those choices, you create consistent character. You get to be consistently you.

What consistencies exist in your character?

What are the benefits of consistency?

Where do you wish to be more consistent?

Enjoy Nature

Lonzo and I enjoy going into the woods, especially at Lake Carlos State Park. Being amongst the trees on natural trails offers Lonzo's sniffer great delight. It slows my heartbeat and brings my mind to the present. Even when the elements prevent long hikes, we enjoy views of the trees or sunrise out the front picture window. Taking time to enjoy nature restores the soul.

Whether you consider yourself an outdoorsy person, something happens when you enjoy nature. You may spend hours hiking, take a swim in a lake or ocean, or simply enjoy the sunrise or sunset from indoors. It may offer you a closer connection to the Earth, a new perspective on life, or some fresh air. Take time to enjoy nature.

Where do you feel a sense of connection?

What parts of nature do you enjoy?

What happens when you take time to enjoy nature?

Share the Sunshine

As Lonzo stretches in the sun, I also find my way to the floor to enjoy the rays streaming through the front window. He lets me share the rug space to soak in the warmth. More than enough sun exists for us both to enjoy it. The sunshine belongs to neither of us, yet we both get to fully enjoy it at the same time. It feels better when we share the rug. Whether we intend to or not, we always share the sunshine.

As the earth holds an abundance of resources, so do you. You have time, energy, wisdom, and experience. You may have ideas about what belongs to who and how much or when to share. As you navigate your time between birth and transition, your thoughts about ownership and sharing may also transition. As you benefit from earthly and personal resources, you may be more willing to share these other resources, just as you share the sunshine.

What are your beliefs about sharing?

What happens when individuals refuse to share?

What does share the sunshine mean to you?

Let Ducks Be

Walks with Lonzo take us by a park with a small pond. Lonzo pauses and observes these critters seemingly floating on water. He does not chase or bark at them. He allows them to do as they do and be who they are. He lets the ducks be ducks.

Humans often have thoughts or ideas about how other humans "should" be or "should not" be. You get to decide who and how you will be. You even get to tell folks the consequences for behaving in certain ways. No human must be the way you wish for them to be. They get to be who they are. This may determine what role they play in your life. Either way, you may let humans be.

What does let ducks be mean to you?

What happens when you let humans be humans?

What else could you let be?

Nudge the Door

Finding a door not completely latched, Lonzo accepts the invitation to nudge it open. In front of him, he beholds fresh territory that he might spend just a moment taking in or he may explore further. An opportunity for another experience awaits if he simply nudges the door.

When you feel a nudge to explore an opportunity, you may take it. It may lead to you discovering your next best personal calling. You are only committing to checking it out for a moment.

You might enjoy it just long enough to discern whether you wish to stay in this new space, go through the next door, or turn around and return to your starting point. It may lead you to a whole new array of opportunities. You do not know unless you nudge the door open.

What doors might you nudge open?

What happens when you explore new opportunities?

What happens when you do not take the chance?

Accept Abundant Love

Lonzo receives unconditional love. Like the love he so freely gives, he also freely accepts. Moments in which his behavior calls for redirection do not change his lovability. He knows that at his core he remains fully worthy of love. Lonzo remains open to accepting abundant love.

You may always feel worthy of love. A part of you knows nothing separates you from love. Another part may feel you must do something to earn it. Not feeling worthy of love makes it difficult to receive love.

You do not have to do anything to qualify to receive love. You remain inherently worthy of love by your human beingness. To allow it to stay in flow, fully accept abundant love.

What does it mean for you to fully receive love?

What happens when you accept love?

What happens when you embrace the love you are fully worthy of receiving?

Embrace the Fullness

Lonzo moves some, plays some, eats some, rests some, and cuddles some every day. He just naturally takes the time for each without looking at a calendar or schedule. He lives life fully. He knows internally to take enough time for activities in all areas. Lonzo embraces the fullness of life.

Life may call for focus on one specific project or activity sometimes. Yet, taking even a few minutes each day for some connection, a little joy, something purposeful, a bit of peace, a healthy activity, or a moment of freedom allows you to fully live. Embrace the fullness of being alive.

What brings you freedom and joy?

Where do you find peace and purpose?

What priority are you giving to your health and relationships?

Generate Gratitude

With another human friend joining Lonzo and I for hike, we forgo our typical path to enjoy the sights of a less traveled trail. Suddenly, brown specks cover Lonzo's creamy-colored fur from head to tail and neck to stomach. I am so happy and grateful my friend does not fret and removes those tiny little wood ticks right along with me.

When you encounter a messy situation, you may focus on your frustration, or be grateful. You may give attention to whatever resources exist to respond and resolve. When you choose appreciation, you change the energy for yourself and the people around you. You generate gratitude by giving attention to the bright side.

🐾 *What does it mean for you to choose gratitude?*

🐾 *Where do you offer grateful energy?*

🐾 *What happens when you generate gratitude?*

Awaken Your Light

Lonzo shines his beautiful light everywhere he goes with everyone he meets. He does so by simply being Lonzo. Many folks comment to me how his beautiful energy brings them joy or peace. The quiet, yet confident critter with mangled hair grows more fully himself each day. He lets his own light shine.

The beautiful light inside of you wishes to shine. That light reflects your sense of inner joy, peace, and love that already exists. The more you allow it to shine, the more peace you will experience. Your light also shines as a beacon for those around you. As you live more as the amazing authentic you, you bring hope and harmony to families, organizations, community, and the world.

What lights you up?

What brings you joy?

What step will you take to awaken your light?

Create the Wonderful

Lonzo gives off an excited energy as though he anticipates this moment to be another wonderful moment. He sniffs here and there as though forever on the verge of discovering the new best. He plays a role in creating the wonderful as he embraces wonder in so many experiences. By recognizing the miraculous beauty around him, Lonzo creates wonderful moments.

You may embrace the wonderful within any given moment. As you express curiosity and interest in the world around you, you might notice the beautiful and deep mystery of the earth and sky. You may delight in the wonder of your own breath and heartbeat. You may marvel at the creation all around you. As you choose who or what receives your attention, you hold the power to create the wonderful.

What level of wonder do you experience?

What happens when you approach life with curiosity?

What does it mean for you to create the wonderful?

Show the Way

Lonzo's love flows to his Grandma Person, Uncle People, and neighbors, as well as random folks at the park or walking down the street. No one needs to do or say anything to receive his love-filled tail wag. He deems the humans he encounters worthy of love by simply being. Lonzo shares love unconditionally because he is a loving being. His love shows the way.

You may choose who or what you love with or without condition. Unconditional love has nothing to do with who someone is or what they do. You simply interact from a place of loving energy. You may simultaneously love both yourself and those around you. Loving unconditionally means loving people because of who you are…a loving being. You, too, may show the way.

What does unconditional love mean to you?

What conditions, if any, do you place on giving love?

What happens when you show the way of love?

Gently Let Go

Although Lonzo may not wish to let go of some random object that does not belong in his mouth, he eventually does. He seems more willing to do so when I gently coax it from him. As Lonzo takes his final breath, I certainly do not wish to let Lonzo go. Yet, his body says its time on this physical plane is complete. It is time to gently let go.

You may have thoughts or ideas whose time has passed. Certain beliefs may no longer align with who you are or who you wish to be. They are not necessarily wrong or bad. They may have proven necessary to your becoming who you are now.

Yet, they may no longer serve you as you continue your journey. As you continue along the path of peace, you choose what to take along and what to gently let go.

🐾 *What ideas or beliefs no longer serve you?*

🐾 *What lessons did you learn from these experiences?*

🐾 *What happens when you gently let go?*

Living the Lessons

Wow! Just like that, here you are. Thank you so very much for investing your time and energy in reading or listening to these peace practices inspired by my four-legged friend, Lonzo.

Lonzo's spirit and energy fill the entire home. His presence brings a sense of harmony and ease to my heart. Even when Lonzo is no longer physically here, I sense his spirit. His loving energy remains in various places and spaces because, during his physical time on earth, Lonzo uplifted peaceful energy.

You too give off energy in the places and spaces you go. Your energy seeps from your heart, mind, and lips. You impact the lives around you. The energy you bring to each moment ~ whether it be gratitude, joy, thoughtfulness, or peace ~ matters.

Your thoughts impact your experience and influence how you show up. You may change your energy, thereby uplifting the surrounding energy at any time.

As I mentioned in my introduction, these peace practices are not one and done. The practice of peace takes practice. Like anything worthwhile or worth repeating, you only grow in peace when you allow yourself time and space. Practicing peace takes practice.

You may pause a few minutes each day to reflect on how you intend to be gentle with you. It may mean setting aside time each week to observe the fullness of your own cup.

As you grow gentler with yourself, you may find it easier and more natural to be gentler with the folks around you. You may return to *Lessons from Lonzo* and reflect on the questions time and again.

If you are anything like me, you may experience a powerful sense of inner peace in one moment and the next, not as much. Keep going. Simply being aware of your own level of peace impacts how you show up in the world.

As you center on who you are, where you wish to go, what you wish to create, and who you are willing to be, this idea of practicing peace becomes more natural. You increasingly fill with peace and become the peace.

As your journey in and between inner and outer peace continues, may you...

Be gentle with you.

Be gentle with all.

Be the peace.

Appreciation and Acknowledgment

When you open yourself and your space to love, support, and guidance, special souls enter your life. While Lonzo certainly invited much love into his life, he also invited more love, grace, and compassion into mine.

I am who I am because of Lonzo and the wonderful humans who join me on parts of this journey.

Thank you so very much to all the humans who took the time to shower Lonzo with loving care throughout the years, especially his Grandma Person, Uncle Ppeople, Howe's Haven, neighbors, countless dear friends, and even random strangers.

Thank you to the Lakes Area Humane Society for delivering Lonzo into my life and Glacial Ridge Veterinary Clinic for their care as he gently let go.

Some extra special humans offered support, love, and guidance in transforming Lonzo's lessons into this book. A special thank you to:

~ friend, author, and healer, Debra Quarles for her patient guidance and generous spirit throughout this process;

~ colleagues, friends, and mentors who generously shared their wisdom, guidance, experience, and support in going for paper to publication, including, Lee Becker, Lenora Billings-Harris, Jasmine Brett-Stringer, Lois Creamer, Jermaine Davis, Candace Fitzpatrick, Cathy Fyock, and Amy Waninger:

~ friends who cheered me along this peace path of life, especially Mary Butler, Tez Gabriel, Kari Greer, Tiffany Helleson, Mandy Stein, Stacy Terebayza, and my Gazebo, Tao, Third Tribe, and U Groups;

~ brilliant and generous first readers, including Michael A. Gregory, Greg Bownik, Steph Osborne, Jim Mogen, Sabrina Marthaler, Amani Roberts, and Dan Terebayza;

~ my Nasdaq Entrepreneurial Center Milestone Circle, especially Carmen Crawley, Whitnie Wiley, Della Washington, and Caitlin West, who supportively nudged me to the finish line,

~ my very patient and wise editor, Ken Wachsberger; and

~ my exceptionally talented cover and interior designer, Lucy Giller.

And, of course, if you are incredibly blessed and lucky, there is always that one human friend. The friend who knows everything about you and loves you anyway. To my dear friend, Katrina McCarthy, who through decades of this journey, even across the miles, remains fully generous and gentle with me. Thank you for the gentle nudges and unconditional love and support.

Finally, thank YOU, the reader. By reading, practicing, and sharing these *Lessons from Lonzo*, you bring Lonzo's peace practices to life.

Thank you for sharing this journey and embracing your personal power to create peace.

Be gentle with you.

Be gentle with all.

Be the peace.

Meet Lonzo's Human
and the Author

As Lonzo's human, Sherry Ann Bruckner, continually navigates her own peace journey, she notices the connection between inner and outer peace as an attorney, mediator, and fully human being.

Sherry Ann has helped thousands of people navigate conflict within their families, organizations, and selves. She serves as a neutral on a variety of civil matters, including bias and discrimination cases; provides transformational coaching, consulting, workshops, and retreats; and speaks and trains globally on conflict resolution, peacebuilding, and transformation.

Originally from Prairie du Chien, Wisconsin, Sherry Ann now calls Alexandria, Minnesota, home. She enjoys hiking, laughter with loved ones, and, now and then, naps.

www.ingramcontent.com/pod-product-compliance
Lightning Source LLC
Chambersburg PA
CBHW070116030426
42335CB00016B/2172